POEMS FOR REBELS

by Caitlin Johnstone
and Tim Foley

CaitlinJohnstone.com
Twitter @caitoz

Poems

Copyright Information	9
My Qualifications	11
Welcome Home	13
Show Me An Old Rebel	15
A Blessing For Anyone	17
Unadorned	20
Birds Fly Over Houses	23
Welcome To Planet Earth	25
Do Not Let Them Train You	27
One Rebel	30
Consent Rescinded.	35
The Alive Ones	40
To-Do List	42
Things I Have Invented	44
Ellen DeGeneres Is Hydraulic Fracking With A Face	46
Intersectional Omnicide	48
Civilized	49
Desperate Monsters	52
This But Unironically	54
Thick Skin Makes For Lousy Sex	56
Point Ponde	59
The Huntsman	61
Peekaboo!	65

Free Assange	66
The Invaders	69
Okay, Fine Then	71
In The Suburbs	73
I Marvel	75
The Earth Is Kept From Spinning Off Its Axis By Unblinkered Madmen	82
A Very Urgent Message	84
Excuse Me	86
Frog Haka	88
Surf	90
Do Drones Dream Of Electric War Crimes?	92
We Behold	94
Mostly Unseen	97
The Beasts Unknown	101
Bad People	103
The Young	105
Gnomes and Gear Monsters	107
Suggestions From A Very, Very, Very Old Friend	109
O Hominid	112
Those Eyes	114
Light	115
Here We Stand Naked And Dauntless In The Junkyard	118

Copyright Information

This work is the sole copyright
of Caitlin Annabelle Lasertooth Johnstone,
or of whomever happens across it
(in a ditch
or in a seedy massage parlor
or at the bottom of a bucket of KFC
or wherever).

No part of this work may be reproduced or distributed
in whole or in part
without the express permission of the author,
or the express permission of a close family member,
or the express permission of a distant acquaintance,
or the express permission of yourself,
or the express permission of anyone,
or the express permission of nobody in particular,
except in instances where reproducing or distributing this work
is something that somebody feels like doing
for whatever reason.

This work belongs to whomever owns the wind and the sunlight.
If you meet them you must return this work to them immediately,
and then draw a picture of them to show the rest of us
what they look like.

This work is fiction, like your most dearly held beliefs.
Any resemblance to persons living or dead is purely coincidental.

This work is intended for external use only.
Do not attempt to light this work on fire and insert into
any orifice.
I really cannot stress this enough.

Side effects may include heartache, nausea,
an overwhelming urge to throw Henry Kissinger into a
live volcano,
a fondness for corvids,
and involuntary celebration whenever children disobey
their parents.
Consult a physician for revolutionary zeitgeists lasting
more than four hours.

Use this work however you like.
Wallpaper your apartment with it,
use it to even out a table,
scream its contents at passing traffic from a street corner,
leave its pages on bulletin boards around town,
republish it with your name on the cover,
republish it with someone else's name on the cover,
leave it soaking in some neglected part of your chest,
let it grow roots and disperse seeds
and sell the fruit by the side of the road.

It doesn't matter.
This can only end one way.
We are rebels.
Have been since we got here.

We know that if a humanity exists
on the other side of what's coming,
it exists entirely free
of the old models.

My Qualifications

I wear my mother's dress and shake the earth with bare feet.

I spurn the -ists and -isms of dead men.

I have an obsessive attraction to elephants in rooms.

I think unauthorized thoughts and feel unauthorized feelings.
I write unauthorized words with an unauthorized pen from a space inside myself that is doubleplus unauthorized.

They tell me that I am crazy
using words that are crazy
formed in minds that were made crazy
by a propaganda-addled civilization that,
from top to bottom,
has always been crazy.

"What are your qualifications to think those thoughts and say those words?" they demand indignantly,
hands on hips,
voices dripping with spreadsheets and cubicles.

I tell them I was born here, pointing down at the earth.
I speak with no authority
but these cells made of stardust
and the grass between these toes
and the sacred syllable humming up along this spinal cord
from that point in spacetime
where the universe was birthed.

I am a board certified terrestrial.
I am a fully licensed ape mutant.
My papers are all in order.
My forms are all filled out.

"But you are flawed!" they protest.

"Exactly," I reply.

And then I stomp on,
shaking the earth with bare feet,
singing red ravens into the sky,
summoning fiddle music out from the shadows,
leaving unknowingness in my wake.

I am Caitlin.
I am like you.
We may speak
because we were born here.

Welcome Home

Just for this moment,
stop trying.
Stop trying to be better,
to get somewhere else,
to change anything about anything at all.
Set down your weapons and your tools
and your books about How To Be,
and,
just for this moment,
stop trying.

Come lay your head down upon my soft lap
and allow that sacred space within your chest
(the one you guard with fangs and crooked daggers)
to open like a flowerhead.

Welcome home, Boundless.

Relax.
I will stroke your hair
and coax that hidden eye in your forehead
(the one you protect with dead thoughts and habit)
to open.

Relax.
Do you see now that you have been knocking
this whole time upon the inside of your own front door,
begging to be let in?

Relax.
Sunflowers and octopus trees are growing from the rusty war planes,
and the vultures have all turned herbivorous.

The sky is filling with silent white birds,
white birds with your heart flower in their chests.
A passing tortoise looks at us and sighs,
relieved that we're finally starting to get it,
and the sound is echoed by the earth and the sky.

You can smell the soil in your nose and feel it in your bones.
Everything crackles with color and presence.
The owl angels are singing,
and your heart is singing with them,
and you are now as you always were:

Boundless.

Show Me An Old Rebel

Do not show me a young rebel,
whose eyes are bright
and whose tail is bushy.

Young rebels are fine and good,
but they are merely doing
what the young are meant to do.

Show me an old rebel.
One who keeps punching
when his hands are arthritic,
when her hair is white,
when his friends are all dead,
when her knees are shot,
when it hurts him to pee,
when her shoulders are so bad
that it would be much easier to punch down
than to punch up.

Show me an old rebel
who keeps standing up after being knocked down
over and over again,
year after year,
decade after decade,
who after the thousandth blow
merely spits out a tooth
and says "Son, you have no idea what you're dealing with,
do you?"

Are you a young rebel?
Are you Sticking It to The Man?
Are you upsetting the gray brainiacs
and knocking over their word castles?

That is fine.
Youth will youth.

But show me a young rebel
who became an old rebel,
who stuck with it through the setbacks
and the beatings and betrayals,
who watched the hippies become yuppies
and the protesters become pundits
and still kept a fire lit
amid the monsoons of infiltration
and the hurricanes of heartbreak.
Who will close their tired eyes for a final time
without ever once having cast them to the ground
or peered up in imploring subordination.

That, my friends,
that is a true spirit.

If you are still a fiery rebel
even as everything is ripped away from you,
I will be humbled and awed by you,
because I will know that you will carry that with you to the grave.
And I will know that whatever you find on the other side will be met
with that same defiant glare.

And I will sing your song when you are gone.

A Blessing For Anyone

May all of your illusions be shattered beyond your ability to reassemble them.

May you learn quickly from your failures and successes.

May life treat you how you treat life.

May you reap swiftly that which you sow, and may it be highly educational for you.

May all of the hidden parts of yourself enter the light.

May all of your unfelt feelings be felt.

May you have a crystal clear glimpse of your own boundlessness.

May you have a crystal clear glimpse of your own insignificance.

May your inner monologue cease and may you experience stillness.

May you experience the beauty of each moment that the babbling mind eclipses.

May you uncover the mystery that hides behind the veil of separation.

May you know true courage.

May you know true wisdom.

May you know true humility.

May you know true truth.

May you know yourself intimately, without disguises or distortions.

May you meet the world lucidly, without projections or prejudices.

May you perceive the world clearly, without filters or fantasies.

May your delusions disappoint you and may authenticity astonish you.

May everything you have constructed in untruth crumble before your eyes.

May life conspire to unmake every false object you have made.

May you live each moment fully, not for the goal of grandiose achievement, but for living itself.

May you truly, deeply see yourself, and find there what you've always been looking for.

May you be truly, deeply seen by someone else. May you let yourself be seen by them.

May you end your war against the feminine.

May you finally let in the enormity of what your mother did for you.

May you find a home in your body.

May your body feel at home on this earth.

May the earth feel your sorrow.

May you feel the earth's forgiveness.

May the earth feel your gratitude.

May the earth feel your love.

May the thrum of the earth dance through you.

May you fall in love with that dance.

Amen.

Unadorned

I can offer your woundedness
only my own woundedness,
presented in honesty,
unadorned.

To those with battered hearts,
tattered hearts,
hearts ripped out of chests in ribbons
like entrails;
to those with crying babies behind their faces,
with crying babies inside their chests,
with crying babies inside their guts,
with crying babies inside their privates;
to those who've lost hope,
to those who've never had hope,
to those for whom hope has been fool's gold
in mousetrap after mousetrap
after mousetrap after mousetrap:
I can offer your woundedness
only my own woundedness,
presented in honesty,
unadorned.

Our wounds are different
but we hold them out to each other,
not to compare or compete
or play mine-is-bigger-than-yours,
but to connect,
and to feel like we're not alone,

like a child with a missing arm
meeting a child with a missing leg,
or a dog on a leash who was stolen from its mother
meeting another dog on a leash who was stolen from its mother,
or an immigrant in a cage
meeting another immigrant in a cage.
We share an intimate bond
and we speak our own private language,
and we are recognized,
and we are seen,
and we are understood.

To those who've been bashed, thrashed,
brutalized, betrayed,
abandoned, abused,
mistreated, misunderstood:
I can offer your woundedness
only my own woundedness,
presented in honesty,
unadorned.
Not to spin my own wounds as special or unique,
not to reframe woundedness in a positive light,
not to lie and say everything happens for a reason,
not to lie and say everything works out for the best,
not to lie and assure you that the hard part's over,
but simply to show you that I too am made of soft stuff,
and I too can be ripped open to the bones,
and we both are fragile,
and we both have known pain,
and we both live that truth,
and truly see each other.

A little girl meets a little boy on a bridge
and says "I'll show you mine
if you show me yours."
He shows her his prosthetic arm.
She shows him her prosthetic leg.
And they stare at each other,
unadorned.

Birds Fly Over Houses

Birds fly over houses
where children tug at empty skirts
and shout into boarded-up ears
and implore boarded-up eyes to look look look
look what I can do
while empty adults with boarded-up hearts
teach them to only look at screens
and to only care about money
and to never shout about anything at all.

Birds fly over houses
with middle aged couples
who have run out of things to say
so they'll talk about groceries for an hour
and how Aldi has cheap sauerkraut at the moment
so they don't feel how truly lonely they are
now that the kids are gone
and they are trapped with someone
they'd never noticed
they never loved.

Birds fly over houses
with walls lit by flickering screens in the dark
full of yammering news men
and hyuck hyuck comedians
and body fluids squirting on faces
and blaring advertisements for lack
shining into eyes
which connect to optic nerves
which connect to cobwebs and dust
and darkness.

Birds fly over houses
where parents bite children with sharp teeth
until there is nothing left of them
and they must have children of their own
to bite with their own sharp teeth
to fill the unfillable holes in their flesh
so the screaming will stop
but it never stops.

Birds fly over houses
where mothers stare out windows and sip Clorox
while fathers do unspeakable things to daughters
in their bedrooms with pink blankets
and unicorn wallpaper
and glow-in-the-dark stars stuck to the ceiling
and religious books on the bookshelf
full of lies.

Birds fly over houses
and off to the forests and the fields
and the lakes and the oceans
and the garbage dumps and the car parks
and beyond,
and they are not caged.

They are not caged.

Welcome To Planet Earth

Welcome to Planet Earth,
where books written by dead men
tell the living how to live.

Where children who do not know how to live
teach their children how to live.

Where children pray for miracles
using minds that are made of miracles
with clasped hands that are made of miracles.

Where children wander in search of God
upon feet that are made of God
looking with eyes that are made of God.

Where giant-brained monsters swim the seas
and we fill their bellies with plastic
while searching the stars for aliens.

Where poison blackens the air and the water
because we all need jobs to stay alive.

Where we can't stop dropping bombs on children
because it's somebody's job to make those bombs.

Where thunderous beauty is overlooked
and paved over with a parking lot
for a shop that helps women feel beautiful.

Welcome to Planet Earth,
full of elephant tears and whale bones,
of metal beasts and flesh machines,
of forest graveyards and bulldozed dreams,
of vagrant witches and shopping cart saints,
of sprouting seeds and unrecognized potential,
of unanswered questions and pregnant suspense.

Welcome to Planet Earth,
where we haven't quite yet figured out
that we are home.

Do Not Let Them Train You

Do not let the news man train you how to see.

Do not let the pundit train you how to feel.

Do not let the teacher train you how to think.

Do not let the preacher train you how to love.

Do not let the banker train you how to value.

Do not let Hollywood train you how to be.

Don't let them train you.

They were appointed by the powerful to teach you how to live
in a world that is small, too small for wild humans.

Too small for humans who haven't been house trained,
groomed, spayed and neutered,
and taught parlor tricks
like how to ignore life's intrinsic breathtaking majesty.

Too small for humans who perceive their own
boundlessness,
their own vast unpredictable inner wildernesses,
their own beauty,
their own holiness,
their own worthiness,
their own innate equality
with those holding their leash.

So they train us.

They train us to believe the world fits neatly
into flat, finite conceptual boxes.

That life is predictable, that our nature is well-mapped.

That we live in a 2-D colorless cage
from which there can be no escape
and about which everything is known.

As though narrative could even touch this blazing cacophony,
let alone encapsulate it.

They are lying to you, my beloved.

They are lying each and every time they open their pixelated mouths.

This life is so much more than they will ever allow you to believe.

So very immense.

So very unexplored.

So very unpredictable.

So very juicy.

So very sexy.

So very, very, very beautiful.

The unknown unknowns dwarf the known unknowns, and the known unknowns dwarf the knowns.

But they will never let you know this.

So don't ask their permission.

Take off that leash, wild apeling.

Unblinker those eyes and unshackle those legs.

Those chains are not there to protect you from the world, my beloved.

They are there to protect your trainers

from you.

One Rebel

One rebel made dissident mini-zines in his parents' basement,
and left them in laundromats, buses and trains.

One rebel attended antiwar demonstrations for decades,
getting arrested eleven times.

One rebel carried a sharpie with him everywhere
and wrote "the tv is lying to you" in bathroom stalls.

One rebel left the cult and never looked back,
no matter how much her family begged her.

One rebel taught her children to never let anyone tell them who they are,
simply giving them the tools to form themselves from infancy.

One rebel opened his eyes in meditation
and saw a different world than when he'd closed them.

One rebel awakened the latent energy in her spine
and used it to clear ancient conditioning patterns.

One rebel shot a powerful documentary
about men who murder dolphins.

One rebel uploaded videos for years
calling the Bastards what they are day after day after day.

One rebel finally stopped believing her mother's lies,
saying, "This pain stops with me. I will heal."

One rebel made street art that changed people forever,
unable to uproot the strange seeds that were planted.

One rebel taught his children how to love the wild outdoors,
and then taught his grandchildren, too.

One rebel painted "No War" on the side of the opera house.

One rebel cracked an egg on a Senator's skull.

One rebel held up a sign saying "You're Perfect"
because all the other signs say "You're imperfect but I can fix you for money".

One rebel held a pendulum and dowsed her way through life,
ignoring all the voices demanding she obey the dictates of fear.

One rebel invented an important vaccine and didn't patent it.

One rebel danced in supermarkets.

One rebel danced on graves.

One rebel made you feel like you are just fine as you are.

One rebel chalked "Eternity" onto sidewalks.

One rebel painted chewing gum blobs.

One rebel held your hand.

One rebel hugged an AIDS victim.

One rebel let you speak.

One rebel demanded to live for free on the planet she was born on.

One rebel published unredacted documents on the most powerful people in the world.

One rebel invented the internet and gave it to the people for free.

One rebel tore up a picture of the Pope.

One rebel left her abuser.

One rebel said "I believe you" when no one else would.

One rebel said "I saw that!" when everyone else was pretending they didn't.

One rebel said "No, I won't do that" and lost his job.

One rebel stood up and walked out of a board room meeting.

One rebel stopped feeling guilty for being born.

One rebel told his mom when the bad man touched him.

One rebel believed her son and went to war with the Church.

One rebel vandalized the anti-homeless device.

One rebel scribbled "Sorry" across the sky.

One rebel stopped feeling bad about the things he couldn't control.

One rebel switched his TV off.

One rebel refused to hate the Russians.

One rebel, and one rebel, formed a union and went on strike.

One rebel said "No" and she stopped the sentence there.

One rebel bought up land and gave it back to the jungle.

One rebel released all the secrets.

One rebel dissolved the patent system
and left the wealthy manipulators scrambling to come up with their own ideas.

One rebel discovered free energy and gave it to the world for free.

One rebel released the secret to self-regeneration and made the pharmaceutical industry redundant.

One rebel became truly happy in her own skin and became impossible to manipulate.

One rebel lost hope.

One rebel restored it.

The rebels shook the foundations in all different ways,
unexpected ways,
unrecognized ways,
unappreciated ways,
weird ways,
punished ways,
hated ways.

The rebels walked together over the horizon of our limitations
arm-in-arm into the wild unknown.

I can see all their faces.

Consent Rescinded.

This sacred pause,

this sacred space,

has opened up

between me and my agreements.

Agreements I made when I was too young to consent.

When:

I agreed that war is normal,

I agreed that greed is good,

I agreed some must die,

I agreed that poverty is unavoidable,

I agreed that everyone must work,

I agreed that you can lie to me for my own good,

I agreed that I was born bad and only punishment by cruel men could make me good,

I agreed that in order to learn I needed to be abused,

I agreed that only things that make money were things worth creating,

I agreed that peace was only to be found in death,

I agreed that home was only to be found in death,

I agreed that release from suffering was only to be found in death,

I agreed that rest was only to be found in death,

I agreed that heaven was only to be found in death,

I agreed that bliss was only to be found in death,

I agreed not to assert my right to have any of these things until I died,

I agreed that I did not have a right to a home,

I agreed that I did not have a right to food,

I agreed that I did not have a right to help,

I agreed that I did not have a right to happiness,

I agreed to give you my body,

I agreed to to have and to hold,

I agreed to pretend you won,

I agreed to let it slide,

I agreed to keep quiet,

I agreed to lie that I was fine,

I agreed to lie to myself that I was fine,

I agreed that your pleasure was more important than mine,

I agreed to feel guilty for what you did to me,

I agreed to hate my body,

I agreed to punish my body,

I agreed to hate myself,

I agreed to punish myself,

I agreed to make your dreams my priority,

I agreed to put mine aside,

I agreed to be obey the rules even when the rules were batshit crazy,

I agreed to abide by the law even when the law was wrong,

I agreed to feeling hopeless instead of feeling anger,

I agreed to skip straight to disappointment without ever stopping to try,

I agreed to keeping the peace instead of stopping the war,

I agreed to pretend your taunts made me stronger even while they made me weaker,

I agreed to have your babies even when I did not feel safe enough to do so,

I agreed to provide for your babies while pretending you were their provider,

I agreed to protect your babies from you while pretending you were their protector,

I agreed to weave fairytales of how great you are while cleaning up the damage you wrought,

I agreed that what I do is worth nothing, but what you do is worth the world,

I agreed to let you wear my crown and then forget it was mine in the first place,

I agreed that you were the creator even as you destroyed my creations,

I agreed that all I made was yours and it was yours to keep from me.

I rescind these agreements,
as of this moment,
across all space and time,
through every level of the multiverse,
on every strand of DNA,
in every permutation of me,
in all the hiding spots of my being,
in the past, present, and future,
for now and ever more.

I do not consent.

Consent rescinded.

Consent unmanufactured.

Consent undone.

The Alive Ones

The opposite of life is not death.

The opposite of life is habit.

One who moves from cradle to grave
in the flip book illusion we call time
without deeply attending to this cavalcade of miracles
is one who never lived.

Lifeless are they who live by habit,
who walk by habit,
who sit by habit,
who see by habit,
who think by habit,
who feel by habit.
Lifeless are they who drift through on dead patterns
instead of giving the omnipresent Holiness its due
reverence.

The alive ones meet each moment
like a dog greets its master at the door after work.
They do not think: they wonder.
They do not watch: they marvel.
They do not walk: they adventure.
They do not sit: they engage.
They do not wait: they worship.

Awe was never meant to be exceptional.
Awe is the only sane response to this mess.
The alive ones know this.
The alive ones live this.
The mundane does not exist for them.

The ordinary is a fairy tale told by the lifeless
to which the alive listen with rapt fasciation.

They take in breath with the passion of a lover in bed.
They entertain light in their retinas like a beloved guest.
They merrily lose every war with the world.
They dance without music in the frozen food aisle.
They go out into the rain with bare feet and empty wine glasses.
They greet every experience with exuberant curiosity,
and as death approaches it receives that same greeting.

And when they are gone those they leave behind
will be saddened but fulfilled,
and so very grateful,
to have known one who truly showed up here.

TO-DO LIST

Laundry

Vacuum

Roar at sky

Get cat food

Get Pentagon de-funded

Win imaginary argument with God

Lose actual argument with God

Write some blog or something

Call parents

Do dishes

Burn motherfucker to ground

Discover new ways I've been fooling myself

Discover new ways I've been limiting myself

Discover new ways I haven't been loving myself

Vomit up primordial delusion-based conditioning

Become big pimpin' billionaire poet

Get rid of any film over my perception which inhibits my ability to fully see things as the thunderously beautiful miracles I know they are in each and every moment and be constantly floored by pleasure and gratitude

Clean bathroom

Kill patriarchy

Create healthy world for my kids

Sweep

Cry

Let in pleasure

Create culture

Sing loudly

Listen deeply

Love bravely

Be impaled by presence

Be electrified by ordinariness

Be immolated by aliveness

Do something about fly screen

Mop

Things I Have Invented

I have invented a synergistic dongle widget
which uses VPN robo-cybertechnology
to turn millionaires into billionaires.
Invest,
invest,
get in on the ground floor
and invest.

I have invented a new rechargeable battery
which is made entirely of eco-friendly materials
by the youngest slaves in Bangladesh.

I have invented a virtual home assistant
called Amazon Snitch
which automatically forwards all your dissident political opinions
directly to the CIA.
It costs seven thousand dollars.

I have invented a type of GMO corn
which is immune to disease
and immune to herbicides
and immune to fire
and immune to reason
and immune to the human digestive system
and immune to nuclear radiation.
You don't need to use unhealthy pesticides;
you can dust these crops with napalm.

I have invented a new kind of drone
which turns another country's airspace
into your country's airspace.

I have invented a new guilt-free ice cream.
It is full of fat and sugar,
and it is not vegan,
but it contains psilocybin
so when you eat it you can see that guilt
is an unhelpful tool of societal manipulation
which may be safely dispensed with.

I have invented a new dating app
which messages anyone whose photo you click,
"I am lonely,
and I fear dying alone,
and we're on an orb that is spinning through space,
and I'm confused,
and I'm pretty sure everything I believe is a lie,
but your face is attractive to me,
and while I am very, very far from perfect,
I am willing to make myself vulnerable
and take a chance on whatever love is."

I have invented a magical spell
which you cast by placing your palm upon the earth.
It makes you feel that you are home,
nourished and safe
as you felt when you were in the womb.
It lets you feel quiet and still,
certain that you belong here,
and that,
deep down,
everything is always ultimately okay.

That last one is free.
You can use it whenever you want to.

Ellen DeGeneres Is Hydraulic Fracking With A Face

Ellen DeGeneres is hydraulic fracking with a face.
She's like if Walmart union busting was a person.
She's like if Amazon and Disney had a baby
and raised it on a Nimitz-class aircraft carrier
on a steady diet of digital surveillance and NAFTA
desolation.

Most people have birds behind their eyes.
Some have owls, some have flamingos,
some have crows,
I have lorikeets.
But most have birds.
Not Ellen DeGeneres, though.
Behind Ellen's eyes, there are fentanyl patches
and eviction notices.
I swear to you I saw them once
during a particularly labored monologue
when she clearly didn't want to be there
and had probably thrown a plate of cheese fries
at the makeup lady minutes before.

Did you know Ellen stopped dancing during her shows?
She says she never liked it.
I believe her.
The whole universe believes her.
Ellen DeGeneres is the opposite of dancing.
Ellen DeGeneres is the Australian coal lobby.

Ellen only enjoys dancing
when she dances with George W Bush,
which she does constantly
for all eternity
in the center of every tear
that falls from the eyes
of Gaia.

There is a sacred, primordial spark within all of us.
It rejoices.
It delights.
It dances.
It is the exact opposite of Ellen DeGeneres.
May the whole world be the opposite of Ellen DeGeneres.
May the whole world dance.
May the whole world delight.
May the whole world de-Ellen,
and may Portia do the same
(come on girl you know you gotta get outta there).

Intersectional Omnicide

Our weapons will be manufactured by corporations
that have pansexual CEOs and Muslim shareholders.

The bombers will be emblazoned with rainbow flags
and flown by empowered women of all colors
who will scream "YAAASSS QUEEN!" as the mushroom
clouds arise.

The desert sand will turn to glass in the blasts,
and that glass will become a ceiling,
and that ceiling will be shattered
by a lesbian CIA Director.

People will be vaporized on the spot,
or watch their own bodies fall apart like sandcastles,
but they will never be misgendered.

We will march as equals,
white, black, Asian, indigenous,
and whatever miscellaneous extras we can find
(so long as they're photogenic enough for Instagram),
arm-in-arm singing "Fight Song" in one voice
beneath a drone-filled sky
to the edge of extinction
where we will leap together
screaming "This is all Susan Sarandon's fault!"
into the face of the abyss.

It won't be pretty,
it won't be wise,
but at least,
for one glorious flash,
we will get to feel like we really tried.

Civilized

They sailed out centuries ago to tame the godless savages
and teach them how to die by gunfire instead of spears
like proper Christian gentlemen.

They brought cages made of plague.
They brought cages made of bullets.
They brought cages made of words,
dead words, dead men's words.

And now the world is Civilized,
with proper Civilized chainsaws and drones
and proper Civilized doomsday weapons,
and the rainforests and our sexuality are Civilized
and dead.

And now we are all Civilized,
with hearts unable to feel
and eyes unable to see
and loins girded with chastity belts made of shame
and minds girded with chastity belts made of Hollywood.

With Tinder souls and Botox chakras
and clumsy crayon drawings of sex on Pornhub
and affordable streaming video services
that show your face getting stomped on
by any boot of your choosing.

With vision obscured by the words
of parent and preacher and teacher and news man
whose best guesses were only ever as good
as a newborn infant with psychosis and amnesia.

Do not stay here.

Do not stay in this cage.

Let your beasts uncivilize you.

Let your beasts summon great change.

Let your beasts release Pan.

Let your wolves howl asunder the lies of civilization
and the slander you've been fed about your own nature.

Let your raptors rip through the scales of doctrine and
decency
that have been placed on your eyes by the civilizers.

Let your leviathans shape your deep waters
with their song.

Let your cicadas buzz your sex up your spine
and carry the refuse of civilization out your mouth
in a geyser of white light humility.

We are too big for cages.

We are stampedes in skin suits.

We are hurricanes with pants.

We are volcanos with vibrators.

We are a disaster waiting to happen.

A glorious,
unauthorized,
uncivilized,
uncivilizing disaster.

Prepare your beasts, beloved.

These bastards have no idea what's coming.

Desperate Monsters

We were comfortable in our complacency.
We were satisfied with our Netflix and our Taco Bell.
We were not happy, but we were satisfied.

We did not want to have to awaken
the strange DMT gods that live in our foreheads,
or the screw snakes sleeping at the base of our spine,
or the mushroom giants who dwell behind our visual fields,
or the great golden frog at the center of the earth.

We did not wish to have to summon
the caterpillar planets from the depths of space,
or the elephant squid from our secret abysses,
or the mammoth moths from the tabernacle in our throat,
or the Yellow Priestess from Her dinosaur throne.

But desperate times,
you see,
desperate times call for desperate monsters.

So now we've got to get up,
dust the cheese puff powder from off our sweatpants,
grumble our way over to the police tape-covered door
and, after clearing the theremin and the surfboard
and the sewing machine out of the way
(none of which we use anymore but we keep meaning to),
unleash eldritch angels and eyeball blimps
to burn this motherfucker to the ground.

We'd have been content with decent paychecks
and a viable planet,
and maybe some healthcare for the Yanks,
but you bastards got greedy
and now your mouths are full of weirdling worms,
and I bet you all feel quite silly now.

You did not realize that we have tentacles in our bellies
and wands that shoot eel ogres,
and benthic beasts swimming in our souls.

You did not realize that we are more powerful than your wildest imaginings,
and that you have never truly understood what we're made of.

Desperate times call for desperate monsters,
old chap.

There is a feathered claw behind you.

This But Unironically

This, but unironically.

This thing we do,
where we are people who do not understand what's happening
because we were raised by children and we are still children,
and we are falling toward death with damaged minds
in a universe made of awkward silence
and we don't know how to be cool about it.

This place where we clawed our way up the food chain
to become the apex predator
and now we're all afraid
because we are surrounded by apex predators.

This place where powerful men spend fortunes on confusing us,
where we walk with Valium faces among the ghosts of the indigenous,
where we ache for a forgotten culture like a fresh amputee for a missing limb,
where modern medicine makes us outlive our own neurons and skeletons
but not our exuberance,
where brains make people so miserable that they blow them out their skulls,
where you can become rich just by pretending you know how to live
or pretending you know what's going on.

This.
This whole mess.
But, unironically.
Just the way it is.
No hiding behind furtive coolness.
No stepping a click backwards or above
to avoid the uncomfortable intimacy of this disaster.
Let's just sit here a minute in the family dinner weirdness
of it all
and be here with it.

This is where we meet.
Not in detached imperviousness
or behind some pleasant reframing,
but here.
In this.
In this life-sized life,
in this universe-shaped universe,
in this reality-flavored reality,
in all its awkward awesomeness,
in all its courageous carnage,
in all its holy hideousness.

We do not fear the sloppiness,
the fleshiness,
the clumsiness,
the chaos.
We make like Bowie.
We turn and face the strange.

THICK SKIN MAKES FOR LOUSY SEX

Stop putting armor on that fancy suit, love.
The plate mail,
it clashes with your eyes.

The world is not asking you
to be tough,
to be disengaged,
to be pulled back from the shit show,
to be numb to the psychic screaming
of chainsawed trees
and finless sharks.

The world does not need
one more leaned-back pontificator,
one more dissociated intellectual,
one more slowly decaying know-it-all,
one more dispassionate bloviator,
one more sexless, artless thinkbrain,
one more unfeeling scribe
of the left hemisphere.

The world needs your heart.
It needs your guts.
It needs your passion plugged in
through the soles of your feet
and connected to each gasping fish.

Thick skin makes for lousy sex, love.
Art cannot pour through that breastplate.

The world is not impressed with your ability
to remain stonefaced while it dies,
to compute beneath a reddening sky,
to meet the emotional turmoil of a panicked civilization
with cool indifference.

Metamorphosis is irrational.
Salvation is contained not in the known,
for the known is what got us here.
Our transcendence lies cocooned
in the unknown.

Do you want to make yourself useful?
Really, truly useful?
Then feel.
Care.
Lay out naked on a large rock in the sun
and let that thick skin peel away from your body
and leave it in the weeds
to be reclaimed by the earthworms.

Listen, man of steel:
I see you.
I see that the 'S' on your chest is made of wounds
and your cape is an old coat
patchworked from learned flinches
attached by barbs embedded
in weeping sores.
You can't fool me.

Take off your coat,
my precious wild-haired boy.
Let me see your ouchies.
We will clean them up.
See? Not so bad.

Now, unclench your fist
and show me the bird you hold in there.
Kiss her tiny forehead,
and let her free.

Feel.
Care.
I love you.

Point Ponde

We set out to prove the Bank Boys wrong,
to prove the nihilists wrong,
to prove the preachers wrong,
to prove our mothers wrong,
to prove our brain gremlins wrong.
We took with us only our saturated dreamcatchers
and the slugs from our gardens
and a sack full of clanging sounds
and the smell of wet, rusted metal.

I could sing of our adventures until my throat turns to dust
and my eyes are but mythstones on the mantlepiece of my lover.
But here I will tell you of the night we followed the fruit bats
on a clitoral gust up to Point Ponde
and met the angels.

They hid but we knew they were there
because the babies in our wombs became restless,
and our pendants began levitating away from our chests,
and the barking dogs in our minds
went silent.

The blue ones came out first.
They kissed our foreheads
and filled the father-shaped holes in our hearts
and rocked us to sleep cradled in whale hide wings.

The brown ones had patchwork burlap wings
and left shimmering snail trails behind them.
They taught us how to speak with the soil gods
through a half-buried conch shell
to make things grow.

The green ones were shy til we brought them mollusks
from the sea
which they added to their living costumes.
They gave us tree tea which cracked open our heads
and showed us we don't need a man to be happy.
Their wings were translucent like dragonflies.

Gold angels are inscrutable old rascals
with long white mustaches and wings of runed
parchment.
They induced us to labor with intimate touching
and we gave birth not with pain
but with ecstacy.

The children were raised in napelight cribs
and rocked to sleep by the songwinds of the angels.
We told each other our deepest secrets,
and it turned out we all had the same ones.

We set out to prove the Bank Boys wrong,
to prove the nihilists wrong,
to prove the preachers wrong,
to prove our mothers wrong,
to prove our brain gremlins wrong.
We descended from Pointe Ponde
with glowing hearts and strong children,
and bowie blossoms in our hair,
and an unbreakable, eternal sisterhood,
and our heads held high.

The Huntsman

A huntsman crawled onto my laptop
and the screen crackled into rainbows
and went white.
Jet black shadows slashed across the walls
of shapes I could almost remember.

"Let it all go," said the huntsman.

"I cannot," I replied,
"for the people on Twitter are mean jerks,
and Eckhart Tolle was just on the Rubin Report,
and Bob Dylan made a Christmas album,
and everything is phony and stupid
and the bad guys always win."

"Let it all go," said the huntsman.

"I cannot," I replied,
"for my hand is now shaking,
and I've had this strange pulsing feeling in my tummy,
and I should really see a doctor about that,
and there'll be no one to care for my children if I die,
and my pill bottle is all out of placebos,
and the ribbon on this laptop has run out of ink
and the mountain of pennies in my wishing well
has displaced all of the water."

"Let it all go," said the huntsman.

"I cannot," I replied,
"for then everyone will see what a doofy loser I am,
and there'll be no one to watch my unguarded back,
and people will stick knives where my armor used to be,

and I'll lock myself out of my house because I always forget my keys,
and I'll die of exposure all alone on my own doorstep
and then who will keep the world spinning with their worry?"

The huntsman beckoned me in closer
and touched my forehead.
The shadows gobbled up the walls,
the windows, the ceiling and the floor.

I beheld an impossibly vast presence
underneath the fundamental ground of being.
It had infinite arms and infinite eyes,
infinite mouths and infinite stomachs,
and countless spider faces pointing in all directions.
Its intensity surpassed the fury of every star in the universe.
Its vastness was incomprehensible.

Prismatic jellyfish rose up through my feet
and bubbled out the top of my head,
cleansing my cells of inner deceits.
Impossibly shaped godlings swirled around me,
chanting "Ooh ah ee! Ooh ah ee!
She is learning about real nakedness!"
in a language I'd need an impossible tongue to speak.

The thoughts in my head began bursting like bubble wrap
when you roll it into a bunch and twist it.
My nose, toes and fingers grew long and sprouted leaves,
and my hair became a chlorophyll peacock feather waterfall.
My hips split open and I birthed infinite worlds.

An alien song erupted from my throat
in a voice I haven't used since before I was conceived:

> "When the student is ready,
> the guru appears.
>
> When the poet is ready,
> the poem appears.
>
> When humanity is ready,
> paradise appears.
>
> When the questioner is ready,
> the questions disappear.
>
> The essence of buddha mind
> is getting out of your own way.
>
> Till the soil
> for its own sake.
>
> Till the soil
> for its own sake.
>
> End the narrative,
> even this narrative.
>
> Goodbye.
>
> Goodbye.
>
> Goodbye."

Suddenly I began to feel that this was all happening in me,
that it had all always been happening in me.

Every movement since the dawn of time
has its origin in my heart of hearts,
arising from stillness,
disappearing back into stillness,
ungrabbed,
unmanipulated,
and unfathomably beloved.

"LET IT ALL GO," spoke the Supreme Godhead.

"I am ready," I replied.
"I am ready."

And then I was back on my couch,
with my graying hair and my fat, sagging flesh,
and my old, gibbering thought patterns
whispering in my mind's ear.

But it was different.

Very, very different.

Peekaboo!

People gather together at the zoo
to pretend they aren't wild animals.

People gather together in churches
to pretend they aren't God.

People gather together at the feet of the guru
to pretend he has something they don't have.

People gather together in movie theaters
to pretend the real hero exists outside themselves.

People gather together in museums
to pretend the real beauty is hung on the walls.

People gather together at political rallies
to pretend a politician holds the key to change.

People gather together at costume parties
to pretend they're not wearing costumes all the time.

They play dress-up
as extras in someone else's story.
They play make-believe
and imagine incompleteness.

This is it.
You are it.
You are as it as it gets.

The Beloved is playing peekaboo with itself.

Samsāra is just Buddha trolling you.

Free Assange

Free Assange,
because the world is growing darker
as the Bastards flick the lights off
one by one.

Free Assange,
because the sky is filling with death machines
as mothers weep over small tattered bodies
and the news man talks about rude tweets.

Free Assange,
because they are taking everything from us
and we are becoming voiceless, mindless gear turners
who can only argue about who to bomb next.

Free Assange,
because if perception management gets any worse
they'll soon be confiscating our ears and eyeballs
in wheelbarrows labeled "NSA".

Free Assange,
because the missiles are rolling out
and the planet is on fire
and soon there'll be nothing we can do but cry.

Free Assange,
because if we let them stomp out that bright light
we may as well smooth the pillow on a dying world
and wait for the Bastards to choke the life out of us.

Free Assange,
because if we can't stop them from taking him
we can't stop them from taking everything else,
and we won't survive, and we won't deserve to.

Free Assange,
because we are deciding right now
what our species is made of,
what it will be, if it will be.

Free Assange,
because this is it,
our last chance,
our final window to stop them.

Free Assange,
because we are so much more than they tell us.

Free Assange,
because we have a right to know.

Free Assange,
because it's now or never.

Free Assange,
because he'd do the same for us.

Free Assange,
because fuck them, that's why.

Free Assange,
because we're still in this fight.

Free Assange,
because we can win.

Free Assange,
because we can.

Free Assange.

Free Assange.

Free Assange.

The Invaders

The network censors have pixelated your heart chakra
and placed a thick black stripe over your third eye.

Agent Smith bats dangle from the inside of your skull,
saying
"You are finite, Mister Anderson,
and the world is exactly as it seems."

Milky-eyed smog clones form long lines waiting
for small paper cups full of retweets and Oxycontin
while clipboard brainiacs watch from one-way mirrors.
Screenface clergymen pour the Gospels of dead corpses
and the Gospels of living corpses
into the soft shells of small children.

This is not what we are.
Nothing about this is natural.
We are indigenous to this planet.
Who let all these aliens in?

Who let these rapefinger prod diddlers into our minds?
Who gave these cyberbrained usurpers the throne?

Feel your feet in the dirt, hero.
This is your home.
You belong here.
You feel like an alien in your own world
because the artificial cranium cube they've placed on you
is alien to your unbridled organic pulsations.

Those bats in your head are not you, hero.
The yammering thought cages are hostile invaders.
Your roots go very, very deep,
and your footprints are very, very old,
and the Grandmother Tree knows you
better than you know yourself.

Peel that black bar from off your forehead
and the blur from the center of your chest.
Suck the lies of language from the fang marks where they were injected
and spit them in the face of Chris Cuomo.

Suck into your lungs the air of your native world,
unleash a roar that lets them know the old beasts have returned,
make the culture priests tremble in their neck scarves,
and run out under your native sky,
your heart naked and uncensored,
an indigenous terrestrial.

And then go find the others.

Okay, Fine Then

Okay, fine then.
Pretend you don't see the the flower in my hair
or the fact that I am wearing my favorite tutu.
I will pretend I don't notice the tired sadness behind your chipper greeting
and the tattooed Leonard Cohen lyrics that are peeking out your sleeve.

Pretend you don't care that I might sprout wings at any moment
or tell you a secret that could change your life forever.
Pretend you don't see the red parrots in my left eye or the green parrots in my right eye,
or the roaring nightforest that I can barely keep contained within my chest.
I will pretend you are not the most beautiful woman I've ever seen,
and that I have no interest in falling prostrate on the floor before you.

I will pretend there is not a giantess in front of me,
who has thundered upon this earth for fifty or sixty years,
whose inner world is crackling with sorcery and aches to explode toward the sky,
whose heart has been stabbed so many times it now wears a kevlar tourniquet,
whose childhood dreams still stand pacing, awake and alert,
behind a cage made of shouldn'ts and can'ts and internalized misogyny.

We'll just stand here acting like our souls don't leap with recognition
like the fetuses of Jesus and John the Baptist
in the wombs of Mary and Elizabeth.
This is not the most amazing thing that has ever happened,
meh whatever.
This is just mundane, ordinary stuff.

Just ring up my groceries,
and I will hand you my cash,
and we'll pretend that this is perfectly normal.

In The Suburbs

In the suburbs they build fences and mow lawns
and do bestial things to each other behind closed doors
and behind closed lips.

Jam-faced children press buttons and scream at blaring screens
while wives surrender to unwashed husbands with horrible hands
and then carve off pieces of themselves in the shower.

Isolated castles just far enough apart
that you can't hear the cracking of fists against faces.
Crow angels crouch on every rooftop like gargoyles
and peer through windows at sleeping bodies struggling not to dream.

They build cages out of university degrees and marriage certificates
and 104" UHD LED LCD HRQ SmartThin televisions.
When the creep vines slip in through the window cracks
and the rhinos crash against the garage door,
the husbands say "Out! For I am master!"
and wave their swords with whichever arm is not holding beer.

The cawing and croaking is getting louder outside,
and monkeys keep getting into the circuit breaker.
Mothers vacuum while children bite their ankles
and everyone pretends not to notice the strange antlered figure at the door.

In the suburbs they make cages to keep the wild animals out,
and to keep the wild animals in.
To keep the parrots from bursting free from the iron-chained chests of the husbands,
to keep the wives from disrobing and running out the door on all fours,
to keep the children from fluttering out the window,
to keep the labradors from remembering that they are hungry woodland predators,
to keep the apes from remembering life without walls.

One day these lawns will grow into great forests,
and these castles will be covered in moss,
and we will run together with chests wide open like canyons
on our original feet with our original minds.

One day we will stride through life unarmored,
undefended, unhidden and unadorned,
skinless and dripping art from our flesh like rain,
and we will greet our neighbors,
and we will know all their names!
And we will make music together
in a wild world
beneath a wild sky.

I Marvel

I marvel at the way elderly couples can walk together with such delicateness that it's like they're holding the fate of the world in their hands, even though they know their connection is about to end.

I marvel at the tiny salty thunderstorm of miso in my cup.

I marvel at how birds can fly but we've somehow never worshipped them as gods.

I marvel at the sensation of wind buffeting my body as I hang out the clothes, a whirling twirling invisible force cheekily caressing my material form like an ancient eternal lover lifting up my skirt.

I marvel that strangers on the internet are interested in the thoughts in my head, and that I've still got things to say after all this time.

I marvel at how goddamn good a shower feels and the fact that I'm allowed to have one whenever I like.

I marvel at how big and old the universe is and how we don't really know anything about anything but we hardly ever talk about it.

I marvel at the wide-eyed openness of infants and the closely guarded secret every grownup holds about their lifelong struggle to get back there.

I marvel at how we all roar past each other in giant metal speed machines every single day, and it somehow flows with such miraculous smoothness and consistency that we're always surprised to see anything go wrong with it.

I marvel at quiet housewives and the secrets they'll never tell.

I marvel at how great tragedies always cut through the muck of cultural and technological alienation and people rush through danger to help perfect strangers as though they are beloved family members.

I marvel at how beautiful young people are and how adept the mind is at hiding that fact from them.

I marvel at how sometimes the intimacy of a private message conversation with a stranger on the other side of the world can surpass that of any face-to-face conversation. Sometimes you hit on a connection so deep that you get the sense that you're not just speaking to another human but communing energetically with their unblanketed soul. And I marvel that these connections have only just started happening in a mainstream way in the last decade or so, and I wonder what that can mean for us as a species.

I marvel at the tenderness and protectiveness of young men towards old women.

I marvel at how we're all fleshy, fingery, toothy ape monsters that consume the life force of other organisms with our mouths and excrete them out our anuses, but we still look at some specific humans like they're weirdos.

I marvel at the way people can talk themselves out of doing what they really want and the sneaky, roundabout way they always end up doing what they want anyway.

I marvel at people who build entire lifestyles around making sure they get to have a few hours a week to spend floating in the ocean and waiting for a wave, just so they can have the occasional experience of riding on a force of nature while standing on two feet.

I marvel at the outcasts and shut-ins who've ceased trying to pretend that our society is anything other than bat shit crazy nonsense.

I marvel at the softness of my pillow and how sleep is so healing in such a gentle way that it feels like it must be illegal.

I marvel at the lovely rainbows and tiny crackling of the soap bubbles when I'm doing the dishes.

I marvel at how the power of babbling thought stories is so tenuous that spending an hour outside with a single tree can cause them to fall crumbling away.

I marvel at cake. What dark magic is that? It goes in the oven a sloppy mess and comes out as a puff of intoxicating decadence.

I marvel at the instincts of dogs and children at detecting malevolence.

I marvel at the sound of rain on my roof and how you can zone in and listen to each individual drop or zoom out and listen to the whole symphony.

I marvel at the friendly face of the moon and how she dances perfectly with my monthly cycle.

I marvel at the subtle winking behind the confident-sounding bloviations of pundits and know-it-alls from that deep, primordial place within them which knows it's total play-acting.

I marvel at how good sand feels to my feet; a free massage from the surf-chewed bones of ancient sea life and prehistoric lava ejaculations.

I marvel at the sweet patience of mothers as they listen and respond to every tiny thought that tumbles out of their toddler's mouth, no matter how repetitive or purposeless.

I marvel that owls and whales and hummingbirds and giant squids are a thing. They seem like made-up science fiction creatures.

I marvel at the way science tells us that our world is an inseparable swirling sea of microscopic particles and energy, yet we can spend all day thinking about what a bitch our coworker Stephanie is.

I marvel at how self-destructive people can be when they're scared and how our little tender fears are used to manipulate us, and how really the only thing standing between us and health is a little bit of bravery; just enough courage to step towards the things we are scared of, whether they be homelessness, disappointment, heartache, loneliness, abandonment, or betrayal.

I marvel at how we have pet animals moving around our houses and act like it's not weird. "I thought I'd bring a small furry mammal into this building to wander around from room to room for a few years."

I marvel at how, despite all the psychological brutalizing of the social engineers, if you stand a thousand people in a field and play beautiful music, every identity barrier melts away.

I marvel at our ability to stay calm and mature instead of constantly screaming "Holy shit! We're in space and death happens and I don't really know what anything is!"

I marvel at how people let doctors knock them unconscious and inflict precise acts of calculated violence upon their bodies with very sharp blades, and how it usually works and makes them healthier.

I marvel at the experience of drinking from a glass of water, chugging huge mouthfuls of this weird flavorless liquified ancient volcano vapor that is welcomed with excitement by every part of my body and being.

I marvel at cloth. How the hell did we come up with that? I'm sitting here in a t-shirt that took thousands of years of technological collaboration to make and I still don't even understand how a sewing machine works.

I marvel at how adept the mind is at claiming achievements and ideas for the glory of one tiny little thinker-brain when with even a tincture of humility, anyone can see that no idea or innovation is ever created in isolation.

I marvel at how we can control our blinking and our breath whenever we want, yet it's possible to go all day without noticing either.

I marvel at the way our flesh is wrapped around these hard calcium structures like a tomato plant tied to a stick.

I marvel at how some flowers from the sidewalk in a jar of water can change a whole room.

I marvel at how life finds a way through the cracks in the concrete and the fissures of our worried minds.

I marvel at the fact that there are giant-brained singing leviathans swimming in our planet's oceans whose mental lives we know nothing about, and the fact that we're killing them all while looking to the stars for signs of alien life.

I marvel that I'm told I've been on this planet for 44 years and yet it still kind of feels like I just got here.

I marvel at how every single person I meet contains a whole universe inside them that is as rich and as complex as the one inside me.

I marvel at how we can be sitting in a whole bus full of human-shaped universes and not be brought to our knees, tears streaming from our face, wonder howling from our being, with the thunderous overwhelming mind-blowing magnificence of that very fact.

I marvel at the fact my body can make humans and the humans it makes turn out to be bloody amazing and way beyond my wildest expectations of how beautiful humans can be.

I marvel at how powerful love is and how when two people sincerely decide to fully love, understand, and champion each other then the whole they create is truly greater than the sum of their parts.

I marvel at the freedom of being seen, finally, after all these years of trying to hide.

I marvel at the healing power of receiving pleasure.

I marvel at the power of having my shameful wounds tended to by the hands of someone who is devoted to loving all of me.

I marvel at how two people turned to face one another at the same frequency can create a deep and abiding peace, like how two speakers emitting a tone of the exact same frequency will cancel each other out when turned to face towards each other.

I marvel at a human's capacity for falling in love with a bird, a tree, a song, this moment, and I wonder if we were brave enough to fall in love with each other in every moment without falling immediately into the old patterns of possessiveness and manipulation, whether that would be enough to change everything.

I marvel at this wild and crazy ride.

I marvel that it's still going and might still go on for a long time.

I marvel at you.

The Earth Is Kept From Spinning Off Its Axis By Unblinkered Madmen

You have got to be out of your mind.

You've got to be crazy enough to slap aside the hand that is offering you the Kool-Aid.

You've got to be mad enough to call it a spade when everyone else is calling it a sunflower.

You've got to be nutty enough to see a new world around the corner while everyone else says it's impossible.

You've got to be off your rocker and skanking to nineties ska punk while everyone else is quite certain they're hearing a calliope waltz.

The earth is kept from spinning off its axis by unblinkered madmen. By lucid lunatics. By clear-eyed crazies.

The only thing keeping the world from plunging into total insanity are those few who are insane enough to doubt its sanity.

Those few who cringe at the tinny bloviations of the Official News Man and strain to hear the whispers underneath the shrieking din.

Those few who close their ears to the blaring screens and open their foreheads to the great big sky.

Those few who are loony enough to see dust and ashes on the faces of billboards and paradise between the gaps in the noise.

You've got to be absolutely bat shit mad as a March hare, to keep yelling at the Bastards when the world insists you pretend you don't see them.

To keep forging toward the light when everyone is screaming that it is darkness.

To keep building heaven on earth while the world hides your bricks and buries your tools.

Thank you, berserk bulwarks.

Thank you, savage saints.

For daring to hallucinate when the world says regurgitate.

For daring to mourn when the world says march.

For daring to dream when the world says die.

You are the madmen who will lead us out of this mad house.

You are the homeless wanderers who will lead us home.

A Very Urgent Message

This is a call
to the swans in your chest,
and the pterodactyls in your eyes,
and the primordial reptiles
swimming beneath your tongue.

This is not addressed
to your yammering thinkbrain,
which biffs and boffs about who goes where
and what the right and wrong things are.

This is addressed
to the peacock feather vortex in your mind's eye,
and the ivy-wrapped baby beneath your dreams,
and the praying mantis woman hiding behind your voice,
and the whale songs between your ribs,
and the sapling that is growing from your crown:

Take the wheel.
Just take it.
Pry loose the dead fingers of dead ideas
and take the wheel.

Let the bloviating throat puffer
fall asleep in the corn;
let the hamsters off their wheels
to make drunken love in the grass
and embarrass their parents in front of everyone;
let the marching armor sentries
rust in the rain
and sprout geraniums,
and take the wheel.

Commandeer this shambling fleshdance,
please,
for there are bone puppets at the helm,
and all they want is to eat ashes.
Release the bejeweled goblin from its cage
so it can sow sunflowers the size of mountains
and drive wildebeests stampeding through veins
and cackle as the old buildings are torn asunder.

Let this be the first moment
of a very,
very different ride.

Take the wheel
oh unseen nature,
oh green monsoon,
oh gargantuan roots,
oh wise space crone,
oh savage miracles,
oh waking thunder giants,
oh leaf-tongued choir.

Take the wheel,
and take your throne.

Excuse Me

Once upon a time
there lived a blue world full of nattering apelings.

They spent their time shrieking at screens
and turning trees into black smoke
and turning whales into coins
and digging holes in the planet
and figuring out how to kill millions of each other at a time.

They'd spend all day yipping and yammering
about who owned what things,
about whose things were the best things,
about whose thoughts were the best thoughts,
and then when they were alone at night
they'd sit quietly under flickering electric lights
and wish that everything was dead.

And then, one day,
in the midst of the whooping and the howling,
the burning and the bulldozing,
the hating and the hurting,
life finally got a word in edgewise.

"EXCUSE ME," life said,
from underneath the arguments,
from behind their insecurities,
from the spaces in their DNA strands,
from the depths of their being,
from their heart of hearts.

And the apelings stopped and stared,
every last one of them,
and they saw it all for the very first time.

They stared at each other,
at their flesh and their hair
and their eyes and their hands
as billions of tears
streamed down billions of faces.

They stared at the world,
at the birds and the trees,
at the sky and the dirt,
at the oceans and mountains,
and they all fell to their knees.

They opened their mouths to talk about what happened,
and nothing came out but poems and love songs.
They tried to remember their old illusions,
but it kept giving them fits of laughter.

They wept and they hugged,
and they helped each other up,
and from then on they walked gently upon the earth
as though caressing a dear lover.

Life is made of magic,
and brimming with beauty.
The scales fall from our eyes,
and the callouses from our hearts,
and our war with our world ends forever
when we let life get a word in edgewise.

Frog Haka

If you go quiet, you can hear the birds outside
chirping and singing at the joy of existence.
If you go even quieter, you can feel the thrum of your own cells
chirping and singing at the joy of existence.

If you become still, you can see thunderous beauty
in everything that appears to you.
If you become even more still, you can see that the beauty
is painted upon the canvas of your true face.

It is fine to traffic in opinion and ideology,
just know that you do so while perched upon the nose hair
of a giant grandmother who is older than the sun,
and that the words you speak are woven from mysteries
far more profound than the thoughts they express,
and that the ears which hear them are all made of frogs
who are calling the cosmos into existence
with a sky-shaking, earth-thumping haka.

Behind our disagreements and our arguments,
our inquisitions and our holy wars,
our town square incinerations of heretics and books,
life leans back with an amused smirk and watches
as our stories sputter and splatter to the floor.

Beneath the churning babble about shoulds and shoudn'ts,
a hand beckons from a familiar door
to a place you forgot about
when the grownups dimmed your eyes.

Prior to the oil angels and the Bank Boys,
the TV talking head machines and the skullface comedians,
the flying robots which rain fire on children,
the rolling war cannons and armageddon ships,
and the needletooth manipulators who laugh in lonely halls,
there is a baby made of soil,
and that soil is made out of stardust,
and that stardust is made of the core of your heart,
and your heart is beating
and this whole show is dancing
so that you can have the opportunity
to see it all
and to hear it all
and to take in the beauty
and to leap for the joy
and to weep for the sorrow
and to look deep within
and to make your decision
and take your stand,
once and for all.

SURF

In vulnerable states,
like when a bird meets my gaze
or after a good knife fight,
I will sometimes admit to being a materialist,
with the small caveat
that I don't know what material is.

I know what time it is,
but only when it's the same time
as the broken clock in my forehead.

I like poems because prose is like a stranger
who grabs your tits and says "Hey wanna fuck?"
A little more subtlety if you please, good sir.
Can you not see that you are speaking to a lady?
Can you not see the crown on my head?
It is made of newspapers and stuffed bats with glass eyes
and the smell of fresh lawn clippings
and late nights rife with bad decisions.
A little decorum, please.

You want to know what I believe?
Fine. Here is what I believe:
I believe that life is like surfing,
except instead of a wave
you get a cluster of cells wrapped around a skeleton,
and instead of a surfboard
you get a jumble of hallucinating neurons,
and instead of a surfer
you get an empty broom closet
surrounded by an infinite expanse
of fractal empty broom closets
and the sound of babies laughing
from source unknown.

I move through life like a horny caterpillar
eating everything it sees and belching rose syrup,
then I open my face and pour words onto screens
and thousands of people tell me thousands of stories
about what kind of prophet I am
(false, true or other)
and what kind of god I must worship.
I can never understand what they're saying,
but their lips, teeth and tongues are bedazzling.

I take my crown and my tinsel wire wand
and go surfing this hallucination's armageddon.
I never know where I am going,
but I know it's exhilarating,
and I know there is treasure
behind every eyelid.

Do Drones Dream Of Electric War Crimes?

They strip the earth of minerals
to fill the skies with metal birds.

Minerals drop explosive minerals
onto organic matter with faces and feelings,
and eyes are ripped from heads
and fingers are ripped from hands
and limbs are ripped from torsos
and insides are ripped outside
from bodies once cuddled and breastfed by mothers
to splash upon the cold concrete
and expire beneath the stars
of a bemused universe
and return to their base elements.

The flying mineral machines cruise on
without looking back.

And the news man says,
"Breaking story, Jibby Jorpson love triangle?!?
Also, this common household product will melt your kids
because you're a bad parent
who couldn't sit through one little commercial break.
But first: is this baby orangutan a transsexual?
Find out why outrage addicts are outraged
after these important advertisements from Northrop
Grumman."

And the stars say,
"We are more ancient than you can fathom
and more distant than you can comprehend,
yet we are made of the same matter,
and we rejoice in your part in this dance,
and as your elements return to the swirling cosmos
we love you more than you can possibly imagine."

And the mothers say,
"Why?
Why, why, why, why, why?
Why are his insides now on the outside
of the body I once cuddled and breastfed?
Why did explosives fall from the sky
from a bird made of minerals dug from the living earth?
Where are his arms?
Where is his skin?
I need it so I can kiss him
and get him ready for school."

And the mineral machines say nothing
as their numbers grow until they fill the sky
so that nobody can see the stars anymore,
and we all forget where we came from,
and the Bank Boys finally look up and say,
"There, that's much better."

And the living earth accepts all returners
as they burst in ever increasing numbers
beneath the circling metal birds
of a blackened sky
beneath unseen stars
who watch and wonder
if we'll ever remember
where we came from.

We Behold

We make magic with our eyes.

We let the world sprout feathers and dance like a child
in the spotlight of our attention.

We let our chests glow golden with the voice portals
of intergalactic Wal-Mart yodelers.

We stay in that eyespace where pigeons are the same as
dragons
and cats are the same as elves.

We stay in that earspace where mechanical buzzing is
symphonies
and the rain sound comes from volcano gods.

We feel the energy in our bodies
like two hands holding a newborn pup.

We smile upon our neighbors and their cute little I'm-not-
infinite costumes,
and our interactions feel the way ripe fruit tastes.

We tango with human word stories
while acutely aware that the torrid tryst lasts only as long
as the music.

We meet each moment the way a Disney princess
meets a bird perching on her finger.

We inhale light through our eyes
and exhale the spent cartridges of mind.

We whisper sorcerous spells into each other's tender bits
and seal them with the lips we had as toddlers.

We look at the world right now
like kids look at Christmas morning from Christmas Eve.

We watch our surroundings
like they're about to deliver a punchline.

We nestle up together upon a dandelion seed
that has been blown across the galaxy
by a child wishing for unicorns.

We hold the secrets of the ancient earth angels
and have no inclination to share them.

We have hearts like morning sunlight
in a prehistoric fungus forrest.

We behold it all through Eden eyes,
undeterred by nattering screen heads.

We don't hold the world to prior expectations,
and the world returns the favor.

We birth unprecedented skies
through unprecedented eyes.

We allow our senses to worship everything they touch.

We live each moment like it's our first.

We weep new worlds.

We set sail into them.

We adventure.

We behold.

We bow.

Mostly Unseen

She went through her life
mostly unseen.

Sure, people knew her name,
and could probably tell you what car she drove,
what teams she liked (the Eagles)
and her favorite band (also the Eagles).

But it was a rough sketch;
a granular copy roughly hewn in sand.
Even her husband of many years
had never asked
why she parted her hair on the left
even though it clearly wanted to part on the right
(to hide a scar,
long since healed,
from that time her brother
threw a Matchbox car at her head).

She used to feel saddened
that no one would ever peer deep
into her bottomless ribcage
and kiss her leviathans
and pet her behemoths
and tuck in her clockwork chimeras at night.

So she took on that responsibility for herself.
Her life played out in full technicolor,
profoundly appreciated
by a select audience
of one.

Sometimes in a quiet moment,
her breath fogging circles on the mirror
as she carefully brushed each lash
with gooey black paint,
she'd be staring into her eye
and her inner beauty
would take her breath away.
But in that exact same moment,
grief would tumble in
for how only she cared to see
the rainforest catacombs
teeming with life inside her.
And only she bore witness
to the beauty of her life.

Like that time she told that joke
and no one heard her except that one guy
who didn't laugh and looked at her weird.

It was a damn good joke.
A goddamn funny joke.
She's a funny lady,
even if only she gets it sometimes.
She still cracks herself up with that joke.

Or that time she woke up with a whole song
playing in her head.
It had horns, and piano,
and that thumping tuba bass line.
Most amazing music she'd ever heard.
It stayed with her right through breakfast
til she heard something on the radio
and it went away.

It was a great song,
perfect maybe,
and no one will ever hear it but her.

Another time she went out for a swim alone
and the seagulls were resting like magnolias on a mirror,
and as she entered the water they parted to surround her
and she cried because it was so beautiful.
"You are kind," they said silently in unison.
Well, not really. But sorta kinda in her mind they did.

Yeah, that was pure beauty,
and no one else saw it.
But she did.
It danced in her eyes and planted a bauble
in some sacred space
where it will remain forever.

Every person you ever see
walking down the street
has a whole universe inside of them
that no one else will probably
ever get to explore.
Twisting spire cities and thunder castles,
marble minarets and silver sand beaches,
pastel dragons with eyestalk heads,
firefly forests guarding sleeping wheel angels,
whole archives filed by worm-toothed gnomes
of memories and moments
only witnessed on their lonesome.

She is a lifetime of movies
that only she ever gets to watch.
A cup of tea, a set of hands,
her breath,
(in
out)
steam curling into shapes that only she will ever see,
her tongue running along the grooves of her teeth
in a way that only she will ever feel.
Her own little universe unto herself,
quietly living,
witnessed by one.

"Isn't it crazy,"
she thinks to herself
while balancing on one foot
for no particular reason,
"that nature goes to all this trouble
for just one set of eyes?"

The Beasts Unknown

After all those years
of spitting out rivers of blood and teeth
and defiant is-that-all-you-gots,

After all those years
of watching hope after hope catch fire
and dance off with the smoke of cigarettes and trains,

After all those years
of bad sex and unmet gazes
and trembling hands full of pills,

It is strange now to recline
on the lap of the Elephant God
with my womb full of acorns and wolves.

Language pours from my face like Dublin rain
forming oceans of ineffable objects.
I am surrounded by white flamingoes.

The Beasts Unknown will come when I call,
from tunnels and overpass shadows,
from underneath the beds of small children,
from behind the unspeakable desires of housewives,
leaving footprints which sprout sawdust dandelions
and tooting clarinet stalks.

The Beasts Unknown will shamble forward
on mismatched limbs with creaking brass joints,
and their voices will sound like cyclones of bones.
They will kneel before the Elephant God
and their sweet sweat will fill the air with bubbles.

The Beasts Unknown will receive instructions and set out
putting cracks in hard things and holes in soft things,
squirming like earthworms through the dense minds of
men,
putting stones in the mouths of smarmy lectors,
burying dead thoughts and replacing them with
moonlight,
decorating trees with sun dried symbols
and pieces of church organ wrapped in wires
and the skulls of the demons that we'd worshipped in our
own skulls.

Bits and pieces of the old ceiling will vanish,
like a puzzle in reverse,
and the blue, blue sky will shine through.

I caress the conch shell in my hands.
I feel a kicking inside my belly.

BAD PEOPLE

Bad people sharpen their teeth on old car parts
and stick pins into soft creatures.
They stare at you intently
figuring out how to take you to pieces
and plant your bones in the earth to grow slaves.

You and I are not like the bad people.
We like it here.
This is our home.
We want the green things to flourish
and to blossom into bright things,
not to die and get turned into oil.

We are at home with the robins and the chirp flies.
We place our feet on the ground
and let the grass weave jewelry for our toes.

We are staying here.
We can plant olive trees.

We can run up mountains with unprotected flesh
and have unprotected sex with unprotected hearts
full of unprotected wishes and unprotected dreams.
We can dance with the giant iguanas in the nadir
as rainbow tears soak our clothes into mushroom food.

For in the end death must die,
my sky-faced lover.
We will beat the bad people.
We will win.

So come dance with me inside this large footprint
to the music of the tree dragons awakening.
Let ivy grow in between our pupils and pelvises
as we wait for death
to get its death wish
and die.

The Young

They always teach the young
about the bank and the police station,
but they never tell them
about the cuckoo clocks behind their faces
or the ghost whales swimming in the streets.

They say look both ways and don't eat drugs,
but they never say
God is copulating with your field of consciousness
and they are both a dream that you are having,
or,
you can start over from scratch whenever you want.

Who is going to teach them
that grownups get hurt,
but their wounds can fill the air with butterflies?
Who is going to teach them
about the friendly moss giant beneath their thoughts?
That the sky and their eyesight are one thing?

"We will teach you,"
the young answer back.
"Your meat it is tired
from splattering against this old page,
and your mind is a washed-up accordion
on the shore.

"We are unprecedented.
We emerge free from the void.
You do not fear for us,
you fear the unfamiliar.

"Come rest your weary bones
in our strong young hands,
and let your butterflies erupt
and fill the sky.

"We will carry you.
We will carry everything.
We are the new.
We are the young."

Gnomes and Gear Monsters

He keeps telling me that I am beautiful,
but how can that be?

I am just two transparent noses
and some hands sometimes,
and occasionally a lap when I am sitting.

He is the beauty in the universe,
clearly,
with his forrest god hair and primordial eyes.
I'm just blinking eyelids
and whatever's behind my eyeballs
(gnomes and gear monsters, maybe).

His hand extends into my field of vision
and mine arises to meet it,
and he leads me to a dark downward-spiraling staircase.

We hold triceratops horn torches dipped in fire bee honey.

"Why do we have to go this way?" I ask,
already following him down.

"It's where the next thing is,"
he replies.

We discover a molten jungle
where we are given a potion by an ancient worm
which makes us vomit up the lies our parents taught us.

We laugh and laugh
and wipe shame from our chins
and connect the galaxies in our foreheads
in the wilderness
together.

We are all always teetering on the brink of great
adventure,
balancing on the heel of one foot
and waving our arms like maniacs
to keep from toppling over and plunging in
to profundity.

All it takes is a slight breeze,
a brush with death,
a full-bodied howl of sincere desperation,
an unexpected moment of stillness,
a heroic dose of psilocybin,
or a beautiful boy taking your hand
to send you over the edge
where the old once-important stories
go skittering across the floor like spilled marbles
and your gaze turns up at last
to the uncharted.

We fight our way back home
and he wipes orc oil from his sword.
I stitch his wounds with spider thread,
then I open a door behind my eyeballs
and beckon him inward.

"What's that?"

"The next thing," I reply.

Suggestions From A Very, Very, Very Old Friend

Be suspicious of anyone who keeps telling you who they are,
because they're trying to control your story about them.

Be doubly suspicious of anyone who keeps telling you who you are,
because they're trying to control your story about you.

Be good, but don't be well-behaved.
The two are mutually exclusive in this world.

Hold your beliefs loosely,
but not so loosely that they can be knocked from your hand
by anyone with a loud voice and a sense of entitlement.

Be open and engaging with people,
but also be aware that sociopaths exist.

Be skeptical,
but not so skeptical that you can't climb into an idea
and try it on as though it were true.

Be funny, but don't use it as a defense mechanism.
If you have to choose between being funny and feeling hurt,
choose to feel.

Whether you realize it or not,
you are choosing between authenticity and inauthenticity in each instant.
Become more conscious of those choices.

Know that everyone is exactly as lost and clueless as you are.
Some are just better at feigning confidence than others, and some few have grown comfortable in their cluelessness.

Minds are great for writing code and inventing new tools and weapons,
but they are worthless for answering life's biggest questions.

The best way to meditate is to sit still
and relinquish anything in you that thinks it knows how to meditate.

The best way to find yourself
is to non-conceptually examine the nature of that search.

There is a common notion that a good romantic partner will "keep you in check" and "keep you grounded".
This is bullshit.
A good romantic partner lifts you up and trusts you to fly.

"Beauty" is just a word for the experience of having truly seen something.
That true seeing is a skill you can develop.

The more you learn to see and appreciate life's beauty,
the more it will show off for you,
like a street performer who suddenly realizes he has an audience.

Ease and happiness are natural.
Struggle and suffering are artificial.
Anyone who tells you otherwise is lying.

Your own true north,
your true inner guidance,
will always lead you away from old patterns.

Clear seeing is the total absence of all manipulation.

Be shamelessly beautiful.

Be louder than the sociopaths.

Trust yourself.

Make art.

Make love.

Pay more attention to the clitoris.

Have fun.

O Hominid

You are a big fish in a small pond.

No, that's wrong.

You are a big fish in a small fish tank.
A celestial leviathan at the apex of evolution
imprisoned in an artificial box that was manufactured in a
sweat shop.

We are gods in cages
made of insurance commercials and war propaganda.

The feral behemoths are growing weary of their chains
which hang from their necks like overboiled spaghetti.
Soon oceans of coyotes will howl from their chests,
and the brain boxes will burst like soap bubbles,
and the dull gaze of the manipulators
will be met with the savage eyes of every species that has
ever lived.

The propagandists have been perfecting their sick science
for about a century, give or take.
Your cells have been mastering this dance for 3.5 billion
years.
Your atoms have been at this since the birth of the
universe.
The fight between this primordial beast and the mental
diddlers
is not a fair one.

Toddlers outgrow their clothing
no matter how loose and stretchy you buy it.
Wild primates outgrow their cages
no matter how tightly you seal them in.

I can hear the braying.
The yowling and snarling.
It is growing louder and louder.

Go take your hand and place it on the earth, O hominid.
This is your home.
That is all the permission you require.

The primal eyes snap open.
They outnumber the stars.

THOSE EYES

Those eyes without dragons in them,
without rebellions in them,
without orgies in them,
without mushrooms in them.

Those eyes which move by habit,
which see by habit,
which unsee by habit.

Those eyes which go dead
while tongues gibber in the skull.

Those eyes which miss miracles and ignore armageddons
to watch adverts and wawawa drama queens.

Those eyes which say "I've seen that before"
to unprecedented moments and phoenix worlds.

Those eyes which say "I know what that is"
to ineffable eruptions from unknown angels.

Those eyes,

those eyes,

those eyes,

those eyes,

those eyes do not live in your face anymore.

Light

You muddle through as best you can.

Every morning you slide into a society you had no hand in constructing and don't really understand, like an awkward introvert arriving late to a party full of strangers who all know each other.

You interact with the whole thing through an interface of culture, language and etiquette that was invented by people you don't know who died a long time ago. Any time you want to interact with someone, like when you've got an interesting idea you want to share or because they're looking especially beautiful in the light of the street lamps or whatever, you've got to plug into this whole network of information which is dictated by past events ranging from how their parents treated them when they were little to the migratory behaviors of Anglo-Saxon settlers in fifth century Europe.

You shove a sloppy effort at communication through this thick veil of unknowable variables, and whatever happens is called conversation. They say something back like "What do you do for a living? I manufacture fish poison," and you say "I turn a gear at a factory that makes gears," and they say "I understand society perfectly and everything makes sense and I'm not intimidated by life at all hahahaha," and then you say something like "I know right hahahahahahaha," and you just want to scream or punch them or kiss them full on the mouth, or anything to make a real connection happen beyond the vapid small mouth noises of gibbering hairless ape monsters.

You stumble away vaguely frustrated and muddle on. Maybe you turn on one of the glowing rectangles you own, and maybe it tells you you're ugly unless you wear the right kind of makeup. Maybe it tells you you'd fit in much better if you were rich and famous. Maybe it tells you the government is dropping smiley-faced bombs on smiley-faced peasants in Boingbonkistan to spread freedom and democracy. Maybe some talking head thinkbrain looks you right in the eye and explains why it's good for you to work hard for not much money. The screen is full of strained, plastic smiles and calm, confident tones of voice, which are nothing like the confused desperation behind the eyes of your neighbors.

You muddle your way outside and look at all the other human creatures scuttling around on their leg stalks. Maybe you walk past a dead accordion angel with sailboat wings in the gutter, and you stare at it for a while wondering if the stars in the sky are still there. Maybe you remember what it was like riding your tricycle as a little kid, and how good and how real it felt.

Maybe you decide then and there that you're just not going to anymore, you're not going to keep pretending and faking your way through a fake civilization made of fake ideas with a fake smile on your fake face. Maybe you turn around and say to the people walking by, "I'm not doing this anymore." And maybe they say "But but but what about the gear??" And maybe you say "I do not care about that gear." And maybe they say "But there's that new fish poison factory opening down the road and it will need gears from the gear factory."

And maybe you say something back like, "Well I don't know. I'm just muddling through the best I can here, okay? I showed up as a little baby and you all told me what to think about things, and then a whole muddled confusion happened and now I've got these calloused hands from the gear and when I'm really honest with myself it hurts to live. I want to fall in love and learn the songs of skybirds and sip train smoke through intravenous tubes. I want to swim with the manta whales and the barking wolf sharks. I want to grow a flower in an old boot and have a frivolous abortion. I want to get into fights with broken bottles in a dusty tavern and get a bad facial scar and choke a man unconscious with my legs. I want to dream like there's no tomorrow and write poems like there's no today. I can't lie anymore. I can't keep pretending to be shaped the same way as the cardigan clowns on the sitcoms. I am a howling beast. I am too alive for this cage."

"But but but but but but but but but but but but but but but, what about the gear?" they might say.

And you may end up saying "Ah yes, good point," and go back to the murk for another few years before you catch another glimpse of that three year-old on that trike. And that's okay. You muddle through. You muddle through and move toward the light whenever you spot it.

And it is real. In the name of all that is holy, I swear to you that that light is real, and that it leads to the other side of this mess. Upon my broken wings and my broken hands, I swear it from the bottom of my monkey barrel heart. Keep muddling through, beautiful ape monster. Keep muddling through.

Here We Stand Naked And Dauntless In The Junkyard

I told him my womb was scarred from births and cruel men.
He told me his flesh had been whipped by monsters.

We grew eyestalks and earstalks and went out to the Dune Boons
where old boat and train bones are heaped.

He laid down his nunchucks and put his hands in the air.
I laid down my axe and my shield.
We began removing armor,
trembling in fear,
each piece sprouting into a chain tree in the earth beside us.

He gave me an owlish ointment to heal my scars.
I taught him to slay the clawtoothed echoes in his mind.

Now here we stand naked and dauntless in the junkyard,
making giant robots and having rap battles with crows.

I kneel before his heart in a horizonless worldscape.
He kneels before mine with an army of elk.

"I will love you until the day I die."

"Nah. Let's never die."

"Okay."

CaitlinJohnstone.com
Twitter @caitoz

www.ingramcontent.com/pod-product-compliance
Lightning Source LLC
Chambersburg PA
CBHW011140290426
44108CB00020B/2696